Your Kingdom Come

New Edition with Discussion Questions

YOUR KINGDOM COME

EQUIPPING LABORERS TO BLESS THE UNREACHED
PEOPLE GROUPS OF THE WORLD TODAY

John Ridgway

Your Kingdom Come: Equipping Laborers to Bless the Unreached People Groups of the World Today

© 2018 by John Ridgway

This book was published by NavGrads International Sdn. Bhd. The mission of NavGrads International is to help advance the gospel of Jesus and His Kingdom in Asia by contextualised publishing in developing discipling and equipping content that is biblically rooted, culturally relevant, and highly practical.

Published in the United States by Tallgrass Media.

To contact the author, email: john@johnridgway.org
Or visit website: www.johnridgway.org

Cover design by Kok-Yiang Khew
Cover Photo from istockphoto.com
Key icon from www.designbolts.com

ISBN-13: 978-0-9997626-1-5

CONTENTS

1   Introduction

5   Key 1 — Rediscovering the Gospel

11   Key 2 — Recovering the Kingdom

17   Key 3 — Reaffirming our First and Second Birth

28   Key 4 — Recognizing that Relationships Define the Church

40   Key 5 — Rejoicing in the Holy Spirit

46   Key 6 — Realizing Our Freedoms in the Gospel

50   Key 7 — Releasing the Gifts

54   Your Next Steps

61   Additional Reading

63   About the Author

ACKNOWLEDGEMENTS

The author is very grateful to the following people who made very helpful contributions: *Dr. Jonathan Lewis, Tim Lewis and his wife Rebecca Lewis, Jim Petersen, Dr. Vijayan, Steve Slater, David Bok, George McBride, Bill Swan, K. J. Joseph, C Thompson, John Travis, Dr. Milton Coke, Abu Mannar, and Dr. Koshy.*

Introduction

Today we are living in a very exciting time in human history. Secondly, and more importantly, we are living in a phase in history in which God is doing something so amazing and so miraculous that it goes beyond our wildest thoughts and dreams.

It seems as if Isaiah 43:18-19 is being fulfilled before our very eyes:

"forget the former things; do not dwell on the past.

See, I am doing a new thing!

Now it springs up; Do you not perceive it?

I am making a way in the wilderness

(new path**ways** in the scriptures)

And rivers in the desert.

(the Holy Spirit [**rivers** of living water, John 7:37-39]

revealing new insights for reaching the unreached

non-Christian mainstreams in the spiritual

deserts of the world.)

WHAT IS THIS NEW THING?

Over the past three hundred years, countless millions have become followers of Jesus throughout Africa, Asia and other parts of the global south. One striking feature of this growth, however, is that it has occurred almost exclusively among tribal and animistic peoples (what we call the world's minor religious traditions). Among those of the world's major religious traditions, such as Hinduism, Buddhism and Islam, very few have ever chosen to follow Jesus.

What is new and changing today is that **recently millions of people from these major religious groups** are choosing to follow Jesus as their Savior and risen King.

This growth is happening largely through family groups and relationally based movements and is taking place in numerous countries among many different people groups in diverse cultural and religious settings.

The most dominant theme of these movements is the Good News of the Kingdom of God, the central theme of Jesus' teaching and ministry. These movements flow through natural family and various other relational networks in the community and are the key to reaching whole people groups.

We see in Matthew 6:33, that Jesus commands us to **seek first His Kingdom** and His righteousness. In Matthew 6:10 he instructs his disciples to pray to the Father:

> "*YOUR KINGDOM COME,*
> *your will be done on earth as it is in heaven.*"

Throughout history many faithful laborers have persevered in seeing this happen and today the Good News of the Kingdom has **COME TO every nation of the world**. But now we sense that God is wanting the Good News of His Kingdom to **GO THROUGH every nation.** In Matthew 24:14 Jesus says, *"And this **gospel of the kingdom** will be preached in the whole world (every unreached people group) as a testimony to **all nations,** and then the end will come."*

What is the role that God has intended for **you** to fulfill in this life? How can you wonderfully experience His purposes for you in helping His kingdom spread among the remaining least-reached people groups of the world today?

One third of the world call themselves Christians, though many need a revival. Another one third live in the same people groups as the Christians, but have not yet responded to Christ. But the remaining one third live in groups that have very few witnesses to the Good News.

Over 90% of these people live in around 521 large least-reached people groups.

In this booklet, we want to help you start on the path towards effectively impacting these least-reached groups of the world where you live today. Where you are right now, there may be diaspora representatives of these least-reached groups like a Muslim neighbor, a Hindu medical doctor, a Buddhist work colleague or a Shinto friend in your university class. You are unsure how to start bringing the Good News to that person and their family.

This booklet will introduce **seven strategic keys** that can help you towards becoming an effective witness and a blessing to these unreached people and their families in your natural spheres of influence.

We also want to help you to reach the great unreached religious mainstreams around the world. Almost 90% of the people in the least-reached people groups live in Asia. About half of these live on the Indian sub-continent.

If God gives you a heart to go to the places where there is no Christian witness, this booklet will help you, as an ordinary but highly committed believer, to know how to proceed.

WHAT ARE THE SEVEN STRATEGIC KEYS?

As we think of the Good News of the kingdom impacting the nations, we will consider these seven keys to help us become more effective laborers in the unreached harvest fields of the world:

1. Rediscovering the Gospel
2. Recovering the Kingdom
3. Reaffirming our First and Second Birth
4. Recognizing that Relationships Define the Church
5. Rejoicing in the Holy Spirit
6. Realizing Our Freedoms in the Gospel
7. Releasing the Gifts

Key 1

Rediscovering the Gospel

G od works in many different ways in many diverse cultures and so there is no simple formula for success. Various aspects of the gospel appeal to different people groups.

The essential ethos of the gospel that has been recovered is that it is in fact an extraordinary **relationship** that we can have with our Heavenly Father and His Son, our Lord Jesus Christ. We can experience all the blessings this relationship brings including forgiveness, restoration of all relationships, joy, peace, purpose in life, awareness of life after death and an understanding of who we are and why we are in this world.

When we invite the Holy Spirit into our lives, we enter into this dynamic relationship with the Father and His Son, our Lord Jesus Christ.

Ephesians 1:11 (*THE MESSAGE*) tells us, "*It's in Christ that we find out who we are and what we are living for.*"

The gospel is not an entrance into a religion. It is not about becoming part of Christianity. **The gospel is not a religion but**

a relationship. E. Stanley Jones once said, "we have to unwrap the Christ out of the Christianity".

In fact, **we are expressions of the gospel.** In 2 Corinthians 3:2-3 (*THE MESSAGE*) we are told that "*your very lives are a letter that anyone can read by just looking at you. Christ himself wrote it, not with ink, but with God's living Spirit.*" From the first day that a Muslim or Hindu or Buddhist friend meets you, that person is reading the Bible *in you.*

It is therefore imperative that your life is becoming more and more like CHRIST. Paul tells the Philippians (chapter 1:20) that it was his earnest expectation and hope that "*Christ shall be magnified in his body.*" Pray that there will be a BIG CHRIST who is more and more MAGNIFIED in your life.

This extraordinary relationship where Christ is living in us is indeed a **mystery** (Colossians 1:27). Even godliness, when I am becoming more and more like Christ, is a great **mystery** (1 Timothy 3:16). And so, this gospel is, in fact, a **mystery** (Ephesians 1:9; 3:3-4, 6-10).

Paul explains in Ephesians 2:14-18 that there is a WALL OF HOSTILITY (Judaism, verse 15) that separated the Jews and the Gentiles.

Religions build walls. But our relationship with Christ breaks down these walls. Regardless of our religious backgrounds, all people can experience peace and oneness with each other in Christ, that the United Nations can never achieve.

In this dynamic relationship, what is our part? God told King Asa in 2 Chronicles 16:9, "*The eyes of the LORD are searching the whole earth to be STRONG on behalf of those whose hearts are FULLY COMMITTED to Him.*" God's love for us is so extravagant. And as our love for Him grows more and more, then the GOSPEL becomes more evident in our lives.

Indeed, as we grow in this wonderful relationship we naturally become **His ambassadors**. 2 Corinthians 5:17-21 tells us that as a result of experiencing this new relationship with Christ, "we *are therefore **ambassadors** for Christ, God making His appeal through us*" and so we implore the people around us to be reconciled to God. Then, they too can enjoy this amazing relationship with God.

My good friend David represents the trade interests for Australia to the Japanese business community. To do this, he and his wife live in Tokyo, have learnt to speak Japanese, are familiar with the trade policies of the Japanese Government, are knowledgeable on the trade practices between the two countries and they seek to understand how they can best serve the Japanese business community.

So, we too are 100% committed to our King and seek to represent Him well to the people around us in a ministry of reconciliation. Our approach is conciliatory and in no way confrontational but very winsome like every ambassador seeks to be.

John Wesley once said, "God can do more through one man who is 100% committed that 99 men who are 99% committed." Total commitment makes the best ambassadors.

But we must be aware that the evil one through his subtilty seeks to corrupt our minds from the SIMPLICITY THAT IS IN CHRIST (2 Corinthians 11:3). The Good News is very profound, yet very simple.

The tendency is to make the Good News complicated and turn it into a set of doctrines requiring an endorsement of some kind. Paul stated in 1 Corinthians 2:2, "*I decided to know nothing while I was with you **except** Jesus Christ and him crucified.*"

This powerful Good News can be a blessing to all people in every sense, spiritually, physically, emotionally, socially and in every other way. It is truly a **holistic gospel**. Jesus went about doing good, healing many people, driving out demons and touching every infirmity of humanity.

Today our gospel must also touch every area of people's lives. It is indeed a **comprehensive way of life** that impacts everything including our families, our relationships, our financial situation, our job context, our influence in the community, our concern for the poor and needy, and our involvement in the social dilemmas and debilitating problems of our society. Above all else the Good News changes us from the inside out.

My Hindu friend Prasad Krishnamurthy in India, explained to me that Jesus was the God of the Christians and therefore not relevant to him as he already had his own gods. It has been stated that there are over 300 million gods and goddesses in Hinduism. Prasad was open to understanding who Jesus was, but he assumed that to know about Jesus, he would have to convert to the Christian religion which was not attractive to him.

I explained that the Good News is a **relationship not a religion** and that as a Hindu he could learn about Jesus without converting to Christianity. He liked this idea and so a journey began where he and I interacted for hours over the scriptures. We were able to get to know his family. We had meals on many occasions. Our family visited his home many times. His family visited our home many times.

Eventually, through our friendship the Good News began making sense.

Over the next few years he and his whole family responded to the Gospel and began to influence many other families in their own Hindu community.

REDISCOVERING THE GOSPEL

Discussion Questions:

Q1. How would you describe the gospel?

Q2. What makes the gospel attractive to your non-believing friends?

Q3. How do we complicate the gospel?

Key 2

Recovering the Kingdom

We are not just talking about the Good News but the Good News of the Kingdom. The importance of **the kingdom** has resurfaced in these last few decades as people have reached out to the unreached peoples of the world, especially the non-Christian religious mainstreams of Asia and elsewhere. E. Stanley Jones was working with high caste Hindus in India. He wrote a book entitled *The Christ of the Indian Road* (1925) which sold over a million copies. Near the end of his life he wrote *The Unshakeable Kingdom and the Unchanging Person* (1972). His work and his writings influenced believers in the 20ᵗʰ century of the overwhelming importance of the Kingdom of God.

In Hebrews 12:27-28 (*THE MESSAGE*), we are told, "*The phrase 'one last shaking' means a thorough housecleaning, getting rid of all the historical and religious junk so that the unshakeable essentials stand clean and uncluttered. Do you see what we've got? An unshakeable kingdom!*" And Hebrews 13:8 says, "*Jesus Christ is the same yesterday and today and forever.*" **The king never changes.**

When we read the four gospels, we are amazed that the kingdom is mentioned about 119 times and is at the center of everything that Jesus said and did.

It was his **message** (Matthew 4:23). It was his **life purpose** (Luke 4:43). It was his focus from the very start of his ministry (Matthew 4:17,23). It was the **theme** of the Beatitudes (Matthew 5:3,10). It was the **center** of the Sermon on the Mount (Matthew 5:19-20). It was the **first petition** in the Lord's Prayer (Matthew 6:10). It was **His command** to us to make it first priority in our lives (Matthew 6:33). It was the **centerpiece** of His stories as He revealed His purposes to his disciples (Matthew 13:1-52). It was the **topic of His final farewell** discussion over a period of 40 days that took place after his resurrection (Acts 1:3).

The importance of the kingdom also comes out in the ministry of the disciples. It was **Philip's focus** in Samaria (Acts 8:12). After 3 missionary journeys, it was still **Paul's theme** in Rome (Acts 28:23). It was part of **Paul's ministry and letters** from prison (preaching the kingdom of God and teaching about the Lord Jesus Christ, Acts 28:31).

What does the bible tell us about the kingdom?

First, it is a **mystery** (Matthew 13:11) and none of us fully understand the mysteries of this extraordinary kingdom.

Second, it is presently **invisible** and thus not easily observed or understood.

Third, the kingdom of God is primarily **relational**. It is the Father, the Son, and the Holy Spirit engaging with us who believe, and with the lost, and it is **not primarily about ideas and rituals.** We don't proclaim "church" or "Christianity".

We proclaim Christ and knowing him more and more brings believers into maturity (Colossians 1:28).

I was sitting on the floor of a large Buddhist temple in Bangkok, chatting with several Thai Buddhist believers and sharing the Good News with their friends. It just seemed so natural. There we prayed in the temple and talked more. I realized that the Kingdom of God is not defined by religious structures or physical buildings, but is very active in the relationships of those natural networks.

On another occasion, I was with my friend George and his Thai Buddhist believing friends in Chiangmai at a very famous Buddhist temple (Wat Umong). We were worshiping God in Christ in Thai Buddhist style and their Buddhist friends who were not yet in the kingdom were asking many questions. We were on their turf and they were very comfortable. Again, I saw how the kingdom of God has no boundaries but goes along the relationships of the community. At the same temple, I saw biblical scriptures on the walls.

Fourth, the kingdom of God is **spiritual** and **not physical**. Romans 14:17 (*THE MESSAGE*), "*The kingdom of God isn't a matter of food and drink. It's what God does with your life as he sets it right, puts it together, and completes it with joy.*"

Fifth, the kingdom of God is **eternal** (24/7) and **not defined by physical markers** such as the institutional church. The "church" is people and is defined by relationships 24/7. The book of Ephesians shows this. John spoke of a physical baptism (Old Testament) but Jesus spoke of a spiritual baptism (New Testament). The Jews spoke of the Passover but Jesus became our Passover Lamb (1Corinthians 5:7-8). Worship in the Old Testament was associated with a building (temple worship) in Romans 9:4, but in the New Testament it is a revolution-ary change in the way we think and live (spiritual worship) in Romans 12:1-2. In fact, everything under the New Covenant is 24/7 and eternal.

In Ephesians 1:3-14, Paul explains the mystery of what God is doing among all the peoples of the world. He is making them all into heirs of the promise we have in Jesus Christ.

God's plan is to make his kingdom visible through many local and mobile expressions of people living in relationship with one another and the Lord, and also with the lost.

Recovering an understanding of the kingdom is essen-tial for us to bring the gospel into the social and religious mainstreams of the world because the kingdom can cross all boundaries. By contrast the Christian religion is not welcome in many parts of the globe.

The kingdom of God brings with it **Christlike holy lives** and very attractive **kingdom values as we live among the lost** in these non-Christian mainstreams of the world.

Many times, my Hindu friends and Muslim friends in India showed no interest in becoming "Christians". Often in their minds, becoming a Christian was like becoming an English-man, since the British brought Christianity to India. In fact, the British built their churches for the British soldiers and Indians were not allowed to enter these buildings. So, becoming a Christian had a bad smell.

But, I explained that Jesus was not recruiting us to a church structure or to Christianity but to His kingdom. Jesus was very clear when he stated in Matthew 6:33, "*Seek FIRST **His king-dom**.*" Conversations could then begin, where we would start to explore the question, "who is this Jesus?"

As we began to read the gospels together, the Good News of the kingdom would begin to make sense. The journey often took quite some time but we could sense the Holy Spirit was gently speaking to the seeker. Jesus wants **all men and women around the world** to enter into His kingdom and to experience an amazing relationship with God himself.

I was teaching graduate courses in Solid State Physics in India's premier graduate Institute when I met a high caste Hindu student who was studying Engineering at the Sathya Sai Baba's college in Bangalore. Through a mutual friend we became friends and chatted about many subjects. My friend Radhakrishnan, told me, "you Western Christians want us to give up everything we hold precious and join a foreign religion". He went on to say, "you strip us of our personalities". He and I began a journey together reading the scriptures.

One day as we were reading Ephesians 2:11-22, Radhakrishnan looked at me and said, "We are equal. I had always assumed that I was inferior to you since I have polluted blood in me because my ancestors have worshipped many Hindu gods for centuries". He had begun to realize that we can all be citizens of the kingdom. So, what was important was not that we were from different religious backgrounds but that after following Christ we were both members of His kingdom. As a member of God's kingdom, he was able to continue living within his Hindu family. His marriage was arranged to a Hindu lady who was a distant relative. He became what Jesus called, "the light on the lampstand that illuminates the whole household" (Matthew 5:15).

Now he is the head of the Engineering faculty of a major university in India and influences scores of Hindu students with the Good News.

RECOVERING THE KINGDOM

Discussion Questions:

Q1. How would you describe the kingdom of God?

Q2. What is unique about the Good News of the kingdom?

Q3. Why did Jesus talk so much about the kingdom of God?

Key 3

Reaffirming Our First
and Second Birth

It is vitally important for every believer to recognize that we have two births, a physical birth and a spiritual birth. The first birth is a physical birth that takes place in a certain place and at a specific time. The second birth is a spiritual birth from above that Jesus referred to when he talked to Nicodemus, and said "*you must be born again*" (John 3:3). Only then would Nicodemus see the Kingdom of God.

In the past two centuries we have assumed that new believers had to leave their non-Christian religious and cultural roots and background. This usually meant isolation from their families, friends and communities. But now we have realized that God is the one who gave people their first birth. "*God determined the **times** (history) set for them and the **exact places** (geography) where they should live. God did this so that men would seek Him and perhaps reach out for Him and find Him*" (Acts 17:26)

For example, a Hindu family born in Karnataka, comes to realize that God was the one that gave them their heritage depending on the place where they were born. Their culture, their religion, their language and their history at birth were all given by God as He determined the **exact place** where they were born. At their **first birth**, they also received a unique personality, physical features, skin color, and family history.

And all this was from God.

Of course, all of these factors have been affected by the fall and God is in the process of either destroying or restoring the nations. Romans 1:18-23 describes the general tendency for the cultures of the world to disintegrate without the redeeming presence of God and His people.

It is therefore very important to understand the person's first birth and to know their **parents** and even their **grandparents**. It is also valuable to learn about **their family history** and **social place** in the society and what are the **particular values** that are important to this family including their **religious, political and social values**.

Indeed, there was a huge struggle in the early church as the Jewish believers assumed that the Gentiles would need to leave their "pagan" culture and enter into the culture and religion and society of the Jews. But the Holy Spirit directed them otherwise. In Acts 15, the Jewish believers agreed that every believer was free to remain in their own context without being required to become "Jewish".

Jesus always respected the first birth of all people as illustrated by the way He went to the Samaritan town of the woman he met at the well and stayed in that context for two days. As a consequence, many Samaritans then believed that he was more than just a Jewish prophet. But they were realizing he was in fact the Savior of the world (John 4:42).

When Jesus enabled the Greek demoniac to experience new life, this changed man who had 2,000 demons in him immediately wanted to join Jesus' Jewish band of disciples. But Jesus redirected him back to his own family in Decapolis (*Greek* Ten Cities), a Greek country established by Alexander the Great, and later Julius Caesar refurbished these 10 cities. We are told in Mark 5:19 that this man not only went back to his own family but he went to all the people in the Decapolis.

As a result, we find a few months later in Mark 8, that about 4,000 Greek men had gathered to hear Jesus as he and his disciples traveled through this same area. This was the beginning of a movement similar to what was happening in Samaria through the Samaritan woman.

Paul respected the first birth of the Corinthians and encouraged them to remain in their context (1 Corinthians 7:17-24), even though that involved pagan temples, pagan worship and sexually degrading practices.

Paul did not affirm pagan deities or sexual immorality but by being in their context and relating to them, Paul was able to bring them to Jesus and His kingdom right where they were. Paul was able to help them experience the living Christ who would change their lives. They would experience the **second birth**. Paul was able to coach them to live well in their messy context without degrading themselves in that chaotic context. They were learning to live righteously in an unrighteous environment.

The **first birth** enables the **mobility** of the gospel. The second birth enables the **purity** of the gospel.

A Hindu family from Karnataka can easily relate to another Hindu family from the same caste in Karnataka, because of their same first birth identity. A born again Hindu family can then bring the Good News to another Hindu family because of their second birth identity. So, the identity of the new believer is now two-fold. He has a **first birth identity** that is physical and also a **second birth identity** that is from above and is spiritual.

A Muslim family from Hyderabad in Andhra Pradesh would see themselves with a Muslim background and part of the Muslim community yet also followers of Isa Al Masih (Jesus the Messiah).

A Shinto family from Tokyo would see themselves as having a Shinto background and part of the Shinto community and yet also believers in the living God.

Typically, the expectation is that Hindus and Muslims and Buddhists must all leave their own context and join Christianity through baptism, a change of name, a change of cultural dress and food, and go through a cultural conversion.

Once it is realized that we are to respect and not denigrate a person's first birth, the gospel becomes free to naturally flow into the unreached people groups of the world, just as it did in the first centuries and whenever these principles have been practiced throughout history.

Jesus once took the disciples for a four-day walk, recorded in Mathew 16:13-20 for a significant conversation about His identity, his role and the role of the disciples, in the most pagan part of Syria (Caesarea Philippi, at the foot of Mount Hermon 25 miles north of the Sea of Galilee).

The ancient name of this area was Paneas, after the Greek god Pan, the location of a huge cave and believed to be the location of the gates of hell. A statue of Tiberius Caesar was at the entrance to protect the people from entering hell. At this very pagan place, Jesus asked his disciples "who do the people say I am?"

This was about 18 months into his public ministry. They replied that people saw him as one of the Jewish prophets.

Then He asked his disciples who they thought he was. Peter replied, *"You are the Christ, the Son of the living God"*.

The people grasped Jesus' human identity but it was Peter who understood his divine identity. And that was only because it was revealed to him by God. Our human identity (**first birth**) can be **outwardly seen** but our spiritual identity (**second birth**) is **spiritually perceived**. As 2 Corinthians 2:14 states, "Now thanks be to God who always causes us to triumph and makes known the **fragrance** of His knowledge by us in every place."

Having established His identity, Jesus then explained His role, and our role in His purposes. His role is to plant His church. Our role is to use **the keys of the kingdom**. We have a set of keys associated with the **second birth** (a changed life, the scriptures, the Holy Spirit, prayer, loving relationships…) but we also have a set of keys associated with the **first birth:** our nationality, our religious background, our social status, our cultural background.

These often contain insights and bridges that lead to an understanding of the living God.

To understand the keys of the kingdom of a particular community, it is important to **master their language** as that often gives clues on relationships in the society and how we relate to different people in the society. Most of all, knowing their language speaks to their heart. Also, we need to be students of their **culture,** their **history** and their **social structure** (clans, castes, tribes, social classes).

We need to be familiar with the **heroes** of their nation and of their community as that tells us about their **values.**

For example, we have John Sung and Ran Yunfei (famous Chinese scholar, writer and essayist) in China, Kanzo Uchimura and Toyohiko Kagawa in Japan, Mahatama Gandhi and Sadhu Sundar Singh in India. We need to understand **the spiritual and ritual traditions** of the people we seek to serve as well as the **civilizational values** that lie at the core of their family life and national life. We need to learn and **respect** these values.

We need not aspire to academic excellence in understanding these aspects but can learn them informally from our friends in the culture noting that perspectives on the religious beliefs and practices will differ from person to person.

For example, in Islam the **Qur'an** has much to say about Jesus the Messiah. In Hinduism, there are many sacrifices performed such as the **Ayudha Puja** that are a shadow of the sacrifice of Christ and the book of Leviticus is a great connecting point. **Mahatma Gandhi's** high respect for Jesus' teaching in the Sermon on the Mount is another natural connection. Modern Buddhism refers to many **biblical scriptures** as can be seen in Buddhist temples in Thailand and Japan. Even when the Emperor of Japan introduced **Buddhism** into Japan in the 6th century AD, it **came with the gospel of Matthew** which is still seen in some temples today in Japan.

Buddhism in China had integrated Christ right into its midst by early believers who brought the gospel in the first and second centuries into China. The Chinese Emperors worshipped **Shang Di,** the one true God and so today there is the temple of heaven in Beijing which is the only Buddhist temple in the world that has no idols. In fact, this temple has a place where the Emperors **sacrificed bulls** and cows to Shang Di on behalf of the people. Other keys are found in the **Chinese characters** that relate to biblical stories.

The Shinto shrines have **two lions** at the entrance with one lion having his mouth open (Ah) and the other having his mouth closed (Um) related to the first and last letters of the alphabet, connecting to the concept of Jesus being the Alpha and Omega in Revelation 1:8. Also **the grounds of the Shinto shrines** are very similar to the Old Testament temple design. Many words in the Japanese language are similar to Hebrew. For example, the Japanese word for "**Sumo**" (Sumo wrestlers) is identical to the Hebrew word for Jacob, who wrestled with God.

There are scores of these keys in every religion that open people up to considering the Good News of the kingdom.

These keys have been given to us and we can use them with great effectiveness.

My friend Bill, who speaks Japanese fluently, and I chatted with Takamorisan in Tokyo, Japan. We were asking about his family, especially his parents. He explained that his mother was a staunch Buddhist and was not interested in spiritual matters. We asked if we could travel the 6 hours north of Tokyo to meet his parents. He was very excited about this possibility and assumed that we would present the gospel again to his parents. His parents showed us typical gracious Japanese hospitality. Knowing that she was a devout Buddhist, we asked if we could see her *Butsudan* where she prayed to the ancestors every day. She excitedly showed us a black ebony prayer stick in the *Butsudan* that had her ancestors' names written on it. At the top of the prayer stick was the "OM/Ah-Um", the Sanskrit character referring to the unknown God in Hinduism. In Japan, the Ah and the Um are the first and last letters in the Japanese alphabet.

At this point Takamorisan was quite disappointed that we were not sharing the gospel with his mother but were rather taking a great interest in her Buddhist beliefs.

But then we began to explain to Takamorisan's mother that the worship she was doing each day actually points to God, (she thought she was only worshipping her ancestors) and similarly to Jesus who refers to Himself as the Alpha and the Omega (the first letter and the last letter of the Greek Alphabet) in Revelation 1:8.

THE MESSAGE says that Jesus is the A to Z. Again, in John 1:1 it tells us that in the beginning was the OM/Ah-Um and the OM/Ah-Um was with God and the OM/Ah-Um was God and the OM/Ah-Um became flesh and dwelt among us. **This was Jesus**.

This was an extraordinary thought to Takamorisan's mother. Then we went on to talk about Matthew's gospel that is still found in certain Buddhist temples in Japan and explained to her that this was her scripture that she could now read and we gave her a Japanese Matthew's gospel.

Takamorisan's mother was totally amazed. We talked about how she could be a pure Japanese following the Japanese traditions but now experiencing Jesus in her heart and life.

Then she would not have to try to find spiritual meaning in her rituals but she could still show respect to her ancestors.

Takamorisan's father had been asking the priest at the Shinto shrine, where he did some gardening once a year, about the gods there, but the priest gave a complicated explanation involving an ancient script. We explained to the father about the significance of the two lions outside the Shinto shrine.

One had its mouth wide open (Ah) and the other had its mouth completely closed (Um) representing the first and last letters of the Japanese alphabet and how this relates to Jesus. He understood what we were saying and it seemed so simple to him. Immediately the father said that he would go back to the priest and give this new explanation about the god at the Shinto Shrine.

Takamorisan's parents were intrigued about our explanation and began to read the Japanese New Testament. It was not long before they began to understand who God is and how they could experience a personal relationship with Him. This was a turning point in their local community as many others were now becoming very interested in how they too could experience the living God personally in their Japanese context without becoming a member of a foreign religion which they distrusted. Furthermore, they saw how we **respected** their religious heritage.

A leading Buddhist monk responsible for this area has since become very interested. His wife has unusual understanding and enjoyed our conversation as we read John 1 with them.

Their Buddhist sect is focused on "**light**" and so John 1:9 (*the **true light** that gives light to **every man** was coming into the world*) made a lot of sense to both of them.

What is happening with this Japanese family as well as others who have come to know Jesus while remaining part of their Muslim, Hindu, Buddhist or Shinto family and community is that as cultural and religious "insiders" they are able to see and explain the natural connections that exist between the gospel and the socio-religious community of their birth.

What we have noticed, in respect to maintaining the purity

of the gospel is that insiders over time transform their beliefs and practices if necessary to be in keeping with the Kingdom and the Biblical teaching. Some of their beliefs and practices are reinterpreted, as in the example from Japan above, others are marginalized and some are rejected. This reinterpreting, marginalizing and even rejecting however is taking place **in** their community and **with** their community.

REAFFIRMING OUR FIRST BIRTH AND OUR SECOND BIRTH

Discussion Questions:

Q1. Describe your first birth. Tell the story of your second birth.

Q2. What is the first birth of the non-Christian friends you are seeking to influence?

Q3. What are the keys of the kingdom in the religious background of the people you are trying to reach?

Key 4

Recognizing that Relationships Define the Church

As new believers begin to relate to their own families and to others, these relationships give meaning to what is church.

As believers grow in their relationship with the Lord, they will need the encouragement of others as they journey through life. The New Testament is full of the 'one another's that described the relationships that make up the church e.g. love one another, pray for one another, submit to one another.

What is the role of the family in the context of the Good News of the Kingdom of God?

The family has been central to the **gospel** right from the days of Abraham, the father of the Jewish nation and all who have faith. God made a covenant with Abraham and his family. It was through Abraham and his descendants that **all the families of the earth would be blessed** (Genesis 12:3). The gospel was **first** announced to Abraham (Galatians 3:8) and in Genesis 12:1-3 we observe that the family was the central focus of this Good News.

The family is also central to understanding the nature of the church. The Greek word for family or household is *oikos*, occurring about 114 times in the New Testament. The Hebrew equivalent in the Old Testament occurs over 900 times. 1 Timothy 3:15 speaks of "the **household** of God, which is **the church** of the living God."

As we look through the gospels and Acts the concept of a "church" is not associated with buildings but rather with a family or several families.

For example, Cornelius and his relatives and close friends (Acts 10:24), Lydia and her household (Acts 16:14-15), the Philippian jailor and his family (Acts 16:33), Priscilla and Aquila and their friends in their home (Romans 16:5), Nympha and the church in her home (Colossians 4:15), Philemon and his household (Philemon 2), and many other examples. We note that in Romans 16:10-15 nine households are mentioned.

We also note that in Romans 16:5 in the phrase, "greet the church that meets in their home" (NIV), the word '*meets*' is not in the Greek. Other translations (ESV, KJV, NASB) more precisely say "*greet the church in their house*" referring to **the relationships in that household.**

Family is also central to the coming of the **Kingdom.**

Both the teaching and practice of Jesus demonstrate the centrality of family life. In the synoptic gospels, this visible expression of the kingdom is often revealed in the context of the family.

In Matthew chapter 8, we see the kingdom coming into the home of the Roman centurion, then into Peter's home, then in the healing of the demon-possessed men who returned to their Greek homes in the Decapolis. In Matthew chapter 9, men brought their paralytic friend, and let him down through the roof of a home where Jesus was speaking. Then Jesus sent the healed paralytic back to his own home. In Matthew's home, Jesus interacted with Matthew's friends, then with the Pharisees, then with John's disciples. Next, he entered the ruler's home. After that Jesus healed two blind men in his home and a demon possessed man also in his home. Eight family homes are mentioned just in these two chapters.

The family is central to **evangelism**. In the references above, the gospel of the kingdom was preached in a family context. Your own home is very important. Jesus said, "*Keep an open house; be generous with your lives. By opening up to others, you'll prompt people to open up with God*" (Matthew 5:16, *THE MESSAGE*).

The family is essential to **discipleship**. In 1 Corinthians 16:15, we are told that "*the household of Stephanas were the first converts in Achaia, and they have devoted themselves to the service of the saints.*" In Acts, we see prayer vigils, meals, teaching and preaching happening in homes. In Luke 10, the disciples are sent out to find a man of peace, one who would invite others into his home. The disciples were to stay with just that family, bringing the gospel to the people present, and not moving around from house to house.

Family discipleship involves many generations. In Matthew 28:18-20, Jesus commanded his disciples to **disciple the nations**, meaning family-clans or ethnic groups. In Deuteronomy 6:1-9, we have the equivalent command to the nation of Israel regarding the **discipling of the nation**. These verses show what that means: the discipling of the families in the nation of Israel, which itself was a family. We are told in verse 2, that this discipling involved three generations.

Understanding how to disciple multi-generational families is strategic today as we disciple the nations or people groups of the world.

Verses 4-9 of Deuteronomy chapter 6 show in detail **how to disciple the family** and ten important phrases are mentioned.

They include, *"Hear, O Israel: the LORD our God, the Lord is one. Love the LORD your God with all your heart and with all your soul and with all your strength. These commandments that I give you today are to be on your hearts. Impress them on your children. Talk about them when you sit at home, when you walk along the road, when you lie down, when you get up. Tie them, bind them, write them everywhere"*.

The NIV Study Bible notes that these verses were called the *Shema* (the Hebrew for "*hear*" meaning "hey listen up") and had become the Jewish confession of faith. They were recited daily by the pious and every Sabbath day in the synagogue. See Matthew 22:37-38, Mark 12: 29-30 and Luke 10:27.

The family is the basis of **leadership**. In 1 Timothy 3:12, we note that a deacon must be the husband of one wife and manage his children and his household well. And those who had responsibility for several families were elders and they were to "manage their own families well" (I Timothy 3:4).

Leadership in the kingdom is not organizational or positional but functional. It did not stem from titles, but from real responsibilities and callings given by God. We note this especially with **apostles**.

In Galatians 1:1-2 (*THE MESSAGE*) Paul says "My

authority for writing to you does not come from any popular vote of the people, nor does it come through the appointment of some human higher-up. It comes directly from Jesus the Messiah and God the Father, who raised him from the dead. I'm God-commissioned."

Part of the role of apostles was to appoint elders and deacons. These elders and deacons were to function very differently in contrast to the institutional church structure where they are acting in an organizational or positional role. Therefore, the personal lives of elders and deacons and the lives of their families were of utmost importance in the context of the kingdom.

The family is the channel of God's blessing. Abraham's faith channeled God's blessing through many generations of his family and into other families. As we experience the second birth, we become members of **God's family**. Then the blessing of God starts to flow through us, into our families and through them to other families. We are all members of earthly families and then we become members of God's family as God's dearly beloved children (1 John 3:1). Both identities are essential for the gospel. God has placed us in an earthly family whom we can influence and being part of God's family enables us to exert this influence.

Once, Jesus noticed a short wealthy Jewish man sitting in a tree. This was a very unusual situation and it is always important to be alert to the unusual. Jesus introduced himself to Zacchaeus and immediately treated him as if he were an old friend by inviting himself to Zacchaeus' home. The crowd was not happy about Jesus focusing on this corrupt tax collector.

But Jesus was interested in this man **and his family**. We in the West often focus on the individual but sometimes forget that every individual is part of a family.

Then Jesus said to this man and his family, "Today **salvation** has come to **this house**, because **this man, too, is a son of Abraham**" (Luke 19:9). Both Zacchaeus' earthly and heavenly family identities were important. When he had Abraham's faith, his family became a part of the covenant that God made with Abraham's family, to be blessed, and in turn bless all the families of the earth.

We had related to Ashok's family for several years and slowly a few of the members of this Hindu joint family had responded. It was a very slow process.

Finally, the grandfather who saw the change in Ashok's life, began to ask Ashok questions. Ashok gave him a New Testament in very easy English, as the Tamil translation was difficult to follow. He read the New Testament in three months and had several questions. He asked "do I have to change my name and change my religion and attend the church and eat the food of the Christians (beef)? We told him no. You are in the family of God when you believe in Jesus. **That is enough**. And at that point you are a member of His family and a part of His kingdom. You are part of the spiritual church. We explained that you do not have to go to a church, **in fact you and others who believe as you do are the church**. He was very excited about these answers and then said, "I now believe in God and His son Jesus Christ".

He gathered his whole joint family of about 50 members and explained that he was still a Hindu (first birth) but was now believing in the living God and His Son Jesus Christ (second birth) who had forgiven him and granted him eternal life.

Immediately after these statements, many family members began to respond to the Good News. Before long, Ashok told me that he believed that Isaiah 60:22 was being fulfilled in his Hindu community and that a *"little one would become a thousand"*.

The basic way people in the first century related to each other was as families and households that included all the natural relationships associated with the family. Those coming to faith in Jesus followed the same pattern.

One of the most amazing households in the New Testament was that of Cornelius (Acts 10-11). His household was one of the first Gentile households to embrace Christ. We see seven natural networks included in his household[*]:

1. His immediate family
2. His relatives
3. His close friends (Acts 10:24)
4. His work colleagues: those who worked with him (soldiers)
5. His work colleagues: those who worked for him (servants)
6. His neighbors (*"respected by all the Jewish people"* Acts 10:22)
7. Those in need
   (*"always helping people in need"* Acts 10:2)

Every person belongs to a natural *oikos* and as the gospel enters that *oikos*, it can be transformed into a spiritual *oikos* and in essence becomes church in that context.

---

[*] Cornelius' household is a classic example of the natural networks of people associated with a household (oikos).

The Greek word **"ekklesia"** occurs 114 times in the New Testament. It is usually translated "church". On three occasions, it is translated "assembly" (Acts 19:32, 39, 41.) The Greek word "ekklesia" originally meant an assembly of people, sometimes used for a legal gathering as in Acts19:39. Usually it was used of people who were called out of their houses by the Emperor's representative to hear the edicts of the Emperor. So, in the New Testament, "church" never refers to a regularly defined meeting or a building but to people in relationship to one another.

However, today, "church" means a building and an organized meeting. How did this happen?

The Japanese scholar Kanzo Uchimura came from a devoted Confucian family. In 1876, he entered the Sapporo Agricultural College in Hokkaido and the Good News was explained to him by William Clark, who was the President of Massachusetts Agricultural College in Amherst and a committed believer. William Clark had come at the invitation of the Japanese Government. It was the first time in 250 years that the Japanese Government had tolerated a Christian presence. Kanzo through the witness of William Clark believed in Jesus and later studied theology in the USA but was disillusioned by the Christianity that he saw.

He returned to Japan and started a movement outside the institutional church which still exists to this day. As a consequence, he wrestled with the concept of *church.*

In his research Kanzo found that the English word *church* derived from the German word *kirche. Kirche* in turn comes from the Greek word **"kyriakon"**, which does not occur in the New Testament, but actually means a religious building.

Today the English word *church* has become syncretistic.

It means both: **believers** relating to one another (biblical meaning), and also a **building**, where organized religious meetings are regularly held (secular meaning).

When the English-language King James Bible was being translated, King James did not want to use the English word "assembly" or "congregation" for the Greek word **"ekklesia"**, as four earlier English translations had done, because there were many renewal movements to Christ that were meeting in homes and were appearing everywhere in England at the time. Some, like the Baptists, were even re-baptizing people as adults. These movements were refusing to join the official Anglican denomination which was under the king's authority.

So, King James issued fifteen guidelines to the translators including the third one that they must use the word *church* as a translation for *ekklesia*. He hoped to discredit groups outside the Anglican church by using a word associated with the Anglican places of worship. He himself was the head of the Anglican church.

The essence of church in the New Testament is people in relationship with God, with one another and with the lost, relationships marked by love.

These entities are the outward expression of the kingdom and can take many and different forms in every context. The scriptures do not prescribe any set form for these entities but there is freedom for people to enjoy these relationships with each other in either informal or formal settings.

My friend David who himself has Malay roots and has influenced many Malay Muslim families introduced me to several Muslim families who were beginning to follow Jesus. It was very exciting to see their love for each other and how they were introducing Jesus to their relatives and friends.

In the book of Acts, we find that the early Jewish believers were known as *the Way* which represented one expression of the church at that time. Paul appeared to identify with it after his Damascus Road encounter with Christ.

Gentile believers were called by others as "Christians" which followed the Roman form of calling followers of a certain person. For example, those of the party of Herod were called Herodians.

In fact, understanding the nature of the church as being informal relationships in a family that relates 24/7, right through to larger gatherings that meet whenever needed, has unleashed the gospel in unprecedented ways.

In our experience, we have found that new believers often connect every morning and pray together and share the word with each other. In other situations, families will connect every Saturday night and encourage each other and share the issues they are facing and pray and share the word with one another.

Many believers in remote areas connect via mobile phones daily, very much like Hebrews 3:1 where it says "*but encourage one another **daily**…so that none of you may be burdened by sin's deceitfulness.*"

This understanding of these expressions of church in the midst of the Muslim, Hindu, Buddhist and other religious and non-religious mainstreams has given these believers the capacity to **determine their own journey, write their own story** and **decide their own destiny**.

These expressions benefit from *alongsiders* from other global communities who add sympathetic support and advice when needed. The *alongsiders* can also connect these expressions to other expressions of the body of Christ in other contexts. We ourselves have been in this role most of our lives.

RECOGNIZING THAT RELATIONSHIPS DEFINE THE CHURCH

Discussion Questions:

Q1. Describe how you understand the church.

Q2. Is your family the church? Are two individuals who relate to each other church? Are two families who connect with each other relationally church? Does the church have to meet regularly or can people relate to others whenever there is a need to relate?

Q3. The discipling of the family in the Jewish nation is described in Deuteronomy 6:1-9. This is how the Jews understood the discipling of their nation. It was for them the Great Commission of the Old Testament. As you think about how the early Jewish disciples heard Jesus describing the discipling the nations in Matthew 28:18-20 (the great Commission of the New Testament), how do you think they understood the place of the family in this new Commission that related to the discipling of all nations?

Key 5

Rejoicing in the Holy Spirit

It is very important for the new believer to discover the **presence**, the **power** and the **perfecting** work of the Holy Spirit. New believers learn to depend on the **presence of the Holy Spirit**, as they **learn to listen to him as they read the scriptures**. Also, they learn to **listen to him during the day**.

"Listen for God's voice in everything you do, everywhere you go; he's the one who will keep you on track" (Proverbs 3:6 *THE MESSAGE*).

We find the new believers learn to get their guidance for the whole of life from the Holy Spirit as they read the scriptures. Many times, they read the scriptures on their knees praying to God that His Holy Spirit would reveal His purposes to them. The Holy Spirit is faithful to **convict them of sin** in their lives and **comfort them as they face difficult circumstances** including persecution that is very real for many of these new believers.

One of the big issues that the Hindus wrestle with, after coming to know Jesus, is what to do about **food offered to idols**

(1 Corinthians 8:1). I was involved with a group of Hindus that loved Jesus, and we were studying the book of 1 Corinthians especially chapters 7-10. They concluded that God wanted them to **remain** in their context (7:17-24). They saw that chapter 8 was giving them the clues on **how to function in the temple** (the good side of their religion) and **what to do about food offered to idols** (8:8). The scriptures also showed what to be careful about in Hinduism that could lead to **syncretism** (chapter 10) and the worship of demons, this being the bad side of their religion.

And they said to me, we understand your role (as an *alongsider*, as someone from outside who listens to us, encourages us and travels in our footsteps) and that is explained in 1 Corinthians 9: 19-23. I was blown away with their insights. Because this is a controversial passage in the Western world, I had read over twenty Western commentaries. None of them had the insights that these Hindu believers were sharing. It dawned on me that these believers were being taught by the Holy Spirit. They understood their own context deeply in a way that no outsider could understand, and the Holy Spirit was teaching them the truths they needed for their situation. I saw how true the scripture is that says, *"the Holy Spirit will teach you all things"* (John 14:26). His educating **presence** is paramount.

It becomes very strategic to have **relevant and easy to follow translations of the New Testament for every unreached people group**. These scriptures need to be very contextual, as well as understandable and accurate in terms of the **language**. The usage of words that are appropriate to the context, versus "Christian" words imported from the West, is very important.

The scriptures themselves need to be very contextual in

terms of their **presentation**, fitting into the local context and not looking like Western Christian bibles with black leather covers and double columns. Many of my Muslim friends who see Western bibles that have a cross on the front assume that it is a sword, just like in the terrible Crusades against Islam.

In the State of Karnataka, India, the Kannada Bible that was translated by German missionaries working with Hindu pundits, had on the cover **Sathya Veda** (true scriptures) written in Kannada. But the current Christian community felt it was too Hindu. The bible covers were removed and replaced with "The Holy Bible" written in English. Immediately the number of copies being sold dropped.

If the scriptures are available in **manuscript form** without chapters and verses (now mostly available from the internet), then the new believer can **catch the flow of the thoughts** and also **the continuing sense of the drama** much more easily. This really enhances the inductive bible study approach where new believers are asked what they see from the passage rather than the deductive approach that gives questions and bible references that guide a person to certain conclusions.

The new believer in Jesus also begins to realize that the **power of the Holy Spirit** is available to him or her in many ways. *"In the same way, the Spirit helps us in our weakness. We do not know what to pray, but the Spirit himself intercedes for us with groans that words cannot express"* (Romans 8:26). *"Tremendous **power** is made available through a good man's earnest prayer"* (James 5:16).

New believers begin to pray for their family, friends, neighbors and work colleagues. They begin to see healings taking place and demons being driven out of people. They start to become aware of a **fierce spiritual battle,** with victory coming often through persistent prayer and fasting. Most of the new Hindu believers in Jesus face vicious attacks from the evil one after they respond to the Lord. They find that it is only as they pray that they can fight off these attacks.

It is also critical that the laborer, the apostle, the *alongsider* and the new believer ALL become **strong intercessors** and really depend on the power of the Holy Spirit to open up the hearts of the people who are searching. **Samuel** was a wonderful intercessor for his people and it is recorded in 1 Samuel 12:23, "*as for me, far be it from me that I should sin against the LORD by ceasing to pray for you.*"

Throughout history the Lord has responded to such intercessory prayers. **John Hyde** sailed for India in 1892. He died in 1912. In those twenty years, he was leading up to four people daily to the Lord. But he spent many hours and nights interceding for the people of India. Millions of people accepted Jesus Christ from the seeds of the gospel which he planted in Sialkot, Pakistan. He died at 46. His key verse was:

"*O Jerusalem, I have set **intercessors** on your walls who shall cry to God all day and all night for the fulfilment of His promises. **Take no rest**, all you who pray and **give God no rest** until He establishes Jerusalem and makes her respected and admired throughout the earth.*" Isaiah 62:6-7 (Living Bible)

I met **Mother Teresa** in 1979 and have followed her journey for many years. She influenced thousands of Hindus for Jesus. She made the statement, "**My secret is a simple one: I pray**." Her habit was usually to pray for two hours early each morning and then to read the scriptures.

In Isaiah 59:16 "God wondered that there were no **intercessors**." In Ezekiel 22:30, we are told that God "... *searched for* *someone to stand in the gap… but I found none."* Every unreached people group and every family in these unreached people groups needs an **intercessor**. Will you be one? Are you an intercessor for your own family as well?

Abraham interceded for his family (Genesis 18:22-33).

Moses, Nehemiah, David and Daniel interceded for their people. Phinehas (Numbers 25:7) stood up and pled for Israel and the plague was stopped (Psalm 106:30). In verse 31 "his descendants will never forget it." **Your intercession impacts generations.**

Thirdly, the new believer begins to witness how the Holy Spirit is perfecting him or her to be more like Christ. "And the Lord – who is the Spirit – makes us more and more like him as we are changed into his glorious image" (2 Corinthians 3:18). The new believer as he or she **contemplates** the Lord's glory is being **transformed** so steadily and so radically that such a life becomes extremely attractive in his or her community.

In Acts 4:13, we are told that *"when they (the Jewish leaders) saw the **boldness** of Peter and John and realized that they were ignorant, unlearned, untrained laymen, they were astonished and recognized that **they had been with Jesus**".*

As the new believers come to faith in Christ and trust in His word, they and their families are able to ascertain what in their culture they should **retain** or **reinterpret** or **reject**. Again, this is the work of the Holy Spirit. Matthew 3:11-12 (*THE MESSAGE*) says *"…the Holy Spirit within you, changing you from the inside out. He's going to clean house (your life, your culture), make a clean sweep of your lives. He'll place everything **true** in its proper place before God; everything **false** he'll put out with the trash to be burned."*

REJOICING IN THE HOLY SPIRIT

Discussion Questions:

Q1. Describe the role of the Holy Spirit in your life today.

Q2. What is the link between the Holy Spirit living in you and prayer?

Q3. The Holy Spirit helps us to retain, reinterpret or reject the various aspects of our culture. Describe how this has worked in your life.

Key 6

Realizing Our Freedoms in the Gospel

The Good news of the kingdom brings a **wonderful set of freedoms** to a new believer. The new believer experiences **freedom from the penalty of sin**. The new believer also experiences **freedom from the power of sin**, although he is still prone to sin. Romans 6 tells us five steps that lead to holiness i.e., know you have died and risen with Christ, reckon and believe this, offer yourselves to God, become slaves of righteousness, and that leads to holiness.

One of the big freedoms of the gospel is the **freedom from the systems** of this world both religious and secular. In Galatians 4:3, we are told that "*we were in slavery under the basic principles of this world*" and then in verse 9, they are described as "*weak and miserable principles*" that enslave us.

In Galatians, we are told that nobody can force us into a religious system like Judaism or Christianity but we are free to serve Christ and one another. In fact, only **when we are free of the system can we live under the system**. The person who is free of Hinduism can live under Hinduism. Paul could submit himself to different systems and situations because he was free of those systems and situations (1 Corinthians 9:19-23).

Many times, **our consciences** are molded by the people who first influenced us with the gospel.

In 1 Corinthians, we are told of four consciences: the **seared conscience** of the unbeliever; the **weak conscience** of the new believer who is still absorbing the gospel; the **legalistic believer** whose conscience is more controlled by law than by grace; and the conscience of the **mature believer.**

In history, sincere believers from certain Christian backgrounds have insisted that new believers in Jesus take on the traditions and regulations of their particular denomination. In the New Testament, there were certain Jews who insisted that Gentiles were required to undergo circumcision and had to obey the laws of Moses like keeping the Sabbath and giving tithes etc.

In the same way, certain Christians today insist that believers from Muslim, Hindu, Buddhist, Shinto and other communities must leave their natural backgrounds and adopt the Christian culture and its regulations, and so rob these new believers of their God given freedom. The conscience of these believers is more controlled by the law and various regulations than by grace. We are all guilty of this to some degree.

A young man from Northern Karnataka responded to the Good News and went back to his community and helped his whole family experience the Lord Jesus Christ. Within a year about three hundred families had experienced the living God.

Shortly after this, a church planting group came along and

told these new believers that they had to be water baptized, change their names, become Christians, build a church and appoint a pastor. The church planting group immediately built a big building with foreign funds and appointed an outsider to be the official pastor. Within a few months Hindu leaders were very upset with this foreign intrusion into their community and came and destroyed the church building. As a result, chaos took place and the gospel witness in this place was ruined.

We confronted this church planting group as to why they were forcing these new believers who were not their fruit to follow the rules and regulations of the Christian community, and asked them to stop their efforts in this area. We insisted they leave the area. The Hindu leaders who were formerly very responsive to the gospel now came and chased these foreign people out of the area.

Paul in writing to the friends in Galatia, was very upset that certain Judaizers from Jerusalem were insisting that the new Gentile believers had to follow the ways of Judaism. He explained very clearly that "*it was for freedom that Christ has set us free*" (Galatians 5:1).

Today certain Christians have taken on the role of '**Christianizers**' who in fact shut down the freedom of new believers. This must be resisted.

In many situations across the globe, believers have realized that they can refuse these pressures. *Alongsiders* have helped to facilitate this resistance. For example, Paul helped the Galatians resist the pressure that was coming from certain believers of the circumcision party in Jerusalem. When such pressure is resisted, the gospel continues to grow.

REALIZING OUR FREEDOMS IN THE GOSPEL

Discussion Questions:

Q1. Describe what freedoms we have in Christ as we become members of God's family.

Q2. How do you help a person from a Hindu, Muslim, Buddhist and Shinto background to maintain their freedoms in Christ whilst living under the constraints of their background religion?

Q3. What elements of Christianity limit the freedoms of the new believer?

Key 7

Releasing the Gifts

In the modern era, the nature of spiritual gifts has been better understood than previously. When released, the gifts can result in an extraordinary growth of the gospel. This is especially true of the equipping gifts of Ephesians 4:11-12 which were given to **equip all believers to do the work of ministry** that the Lord wants us to accomplish.[*]

The gospel is kept from spreading if we turn the gift of pastoring or shepherding into a position of authority over the other gifts. Such a tendency has been reinforced by seminaries that arose during the Counter-Reformation by the Catholics, and later by the newly formed Protestant communities who also developed these places of authority.

Today these different Protestant seminaries hold numerous

---

[*] You can go to the internet to: **www.theforgottenways.org/what-is-apest.aspx** For $10 you will receive a comprehensive personal assessment of your gifting that gives details on your equipping gift profile that will help you recognize your role in an apostolic team.

conflicting doctrinal positions. A new denomination is being birthed every two and a half days. Authoritarian approaches to leadership contribute to this proliferation of denominations. **Servant leadership based on spiritual gifts is the needed alternative.**

However, there has been a new recognition of the gifts of apostle, prophet and evangelist. These three gifts are primarily needed for the expansion of the gospel in the unreached world.

The **apostles** have the unique burden to "*preach the Gospel where Christ has not been named*" (Romans 15:20). They are able to put themselves in another person's shoes and be a Greek to the Greeks. They understand other people's contexts and how the gospel can make sense there.

Prophets discern the endemic sins in that new unreached context and are able to encourage people to walk in God's ways and live transformed lives. They can also help new believers in Christ see the unique future pathways that the Lord has for them.

Evangelists quickly win others to Christ, usually in their own culture, but across cultures as well. They make the gospel easy to understand for the seeking person and help the person start the journey of responding to the Lord.

These three gifts encourage the new believers to remain where they are, to live among the lost and to disciple the lost. The gifts of shepherding and teaching are needed to enable new believers to grow strong, to work through difficult relationships and to be built up in the faith.

In the Old Testament, the focus was on the nation of Israel being a light to the nations and nations came to Israel to see the God of the Israelites. The Queen of Sheba came to see King

Solomon and witness the glory of his God. But in the New Testament the focus is **not on coming but on going.**

It is easy for Christians to settle into the Old Testament model of inviting their non-Christian friends to come to "church" rather than going to their context, being on their turf and understanding their context. Jesus entered our context in order to help us know the Good News. **Jesus came to seek and save the lost,** Luke 19:10.

As we deploy these gifts of apostle, prophet and evangelist, the gospel is unleashed among the unreached peoples of the world. If our focus is only on church and the stabilizing of the church, we eventually die. Reaching the unreached breathes new life into the people of God everywhere.

All of these factors are equally important under the guidance of the Holy Spirit. There will be other factors that will become evident as we start this journey. However, these seven strategic keys as introduced and explained can be our immediate focus.

RELEASING THE GIFTS

Discussion Questions:

Q1. What are your gifts?

(You can check at **www.theforgottenways.org/what-is-apest.aspx**)

Q2. Are you able to exercise your gifting in your context?

Q3. We understand the role of the pastor. What roles do apostles, prophets, and evangelists exercise in your context today?

Your Next Steps

What is it that God wants you to do? There appears to be at least three options in front of each one of us:

FIRST, be a bringer of blessing, a laborer in the harvest where you are. Make a list of all your family members, relatives, colleagues at work, neighbors, social friends and those in need and begin to pray over them asking the Lord "what is the next step?". God will most likely lay several people on your heart and now you begin to ask, what is the next step in the relationship e.g. send a text, make a phone call, send a birthday gift, etc.

SCRATCH WHERE IT ITCHES. Serve the person where they are hurting. Serve the person continually and at the right time they will warm up to your ongoing friendship.

Help them and their family together take the first steps in following Jesus. Stay with them as they enter the kingdom and help them to begin to influence other families, relatives, friends, work colleagues, neighbors and those in need through all their natural networks. This is a life time journey with our families and relatives.

Paul's family as recorded in scripture seems to have been at least eight relatives with six of them mentioned in Romans 16 and his sister and her son mentioned in Acts 23:16. And we also need to go beyond our immediate families and make special efforts to befriend and relate to people from another cultural and religious tradition.

SECOND, make a physical move to locate in the Hindu, Muslim, Buddhist or secular community in your city or country. You can start attending their religious functions and festivals.

You could also join a beginner's class at their place of worship to learn the essence of their traditions and so understand their beliefs as well as meeting people. This shows a commitment to learn their way of thinking and understand what is important to them. Ask God for insight on how to speak about Jesus in a natural way instead of forcing them into a religious institution or making them uncomfortable with religious dogma.

If you cannot move to a non-Christian community, then spend much of your time in that community drinking coffee in their coffee shops and attending their community events.

Eventually most of your social friendships could be in this new location by joining a sports club, becoming part of a reading group, contributing to local needs, volunteering in the local council, etc.

Wherever you are, be hospitable. Invite your neighbors over. Be alert to their dietary restrictions and ask them before inviting them to come. Look for practical ways to help people.

Respect the first birth of the community. Become a learner and ask questions. Relate to **whole families** and slowly become a member of the community.

Communicate the Good News in terms of good news.

Demonstrate, and in due course explain, the blessing of experiencing God personally and directly and discovering His wonderful ways for our lives rather than focus on the sinner/death/hell approach. We are not negating these truths but we are wanting the Good News of the gospel to be our central emphasis.

Do not criticize their religion but rather look for common understandings.

Utilize copies of passages of scripture without chapters and verses. Avoid big black bibles with golden tails. Read the gospels with them and enjoy the journey.

Often, I ask the question, "**would you be interested to start a journey of figuring out who is Jesus**?" Usually the response is, "what do you mean?" At that point, I pull out two easy to read gospels of John and I have the person read one page and I read the next page and I ask, "**What did you like about what you have read?**"

And so, we exchange a few thoughts without getting into any arguments or me trying to teach or correct the person. And so, we set a time to do this over a coffee or tea and begin a weekly discovery process. This will continue for many months as we read through the whole New Testament and this is better if it can be done with the whole family.

Enjoy people and be relaxed. Avoid comments on any cultural features that seem strange to you. Again, be alert to the seven strategic keys listed above and how they relate to your new unreached context.

THIRD, you could consider moving overseas into one of the mainstream nations that is filled with the least-reached people groups e.g. India, Indonesia, Thailand, Central Asia, the Middle East or North Africa. You can take a job there.

You can get involved in an important needy cause for a certain unreached people group. You can retire to a place with few witnesses if you are older. **Always consider carefully,** how what you might do will lead to you blessing whole families in a natural context. Try not to get involved with things that split families apart or empower part of the family at the expense of the rest.

Getting a job has the advantage that you are not trying to raise money, and as a professional, you will automatically have a network of people in your work place immediately. A job which requires forming relationships is better than a quiet desk job. This is a big advantage because as an outsider it takes quite a while to be accepted. If you have a neutral platform, then usually people are not suspicious of you. Rather they will judge you on your performance.

As a result, we need professional people at every level of society. We need professional business people. We need professional consultants. We need top engineers and geologists especially where oil and gas are being extracted from the sea.

We need professional writers and professional commentators of all kinds. We need doctors and dentists and nurses. We need professional agriculturists and horticultural specialists. We need specialists in law enforcement and International Conflict and Security. We need people who will use their professional skills to serve and add value to the country.

Education is highly valued. Therefore, choose to teach

subjects that are in high demand such as computer skills or English. Or you may become a student learning the language or doing a PhD or other graduate studies in fields that are in high demand in that country. You can also start schools or an educational network of training trainers. But if they see you as a missionary paid to make converts, they will usually avoid you.

You can also raise support for working with a non- profit organization e.g., working in India with an Indian school that helps families of autistic children.

There are many situations where a full-time person would be appropriate, especially in situations where the physical needs of the community are being met by the person. Depending on the country, this can be especially true in the medical field or where the community desperately needs wells, skills in planting crops, construction of simple housing or schooling.

We have friends working with local farmers in the hills of Honduras to help them construct their own water supplies. Consequently, the farmers have become very responsive to the gospel. You can help people bring their native skills or products to market.

Toyohiko Kagawa understood these principles back in 1936 regarding the development of cooperatives for the farmers in Japan and saw tremendous response to the gospel. His book **Brotherhood Economics** is a classic in understanding economic principles in the context of the Kingdom of God.

But seek to do this with **some friends who will pray with you**. And it is usually very **helpful to have a coach** who can guide you and link you up with fellow travelers. Look for a team that has the APEST (apostle, prophet, evangelist, shepherd, teacher) way of thinking.

Also, you may wish to **form your own small society**, team or mobile band that will provide accountability and flexibility that is not always available with large existing mission societies.

This is what William Carey did back in 1792 when he formed the voluntary Baptist Missionary Society of fourteen people, including those going and those staying back, similar to a private trading company.

In the forty years prior to 1792, there were no mission agencies. In the 40 years following 1792, eleven societies came into being from all over the Western world, inspired by Carey.

A CALL TO ACTION

WOULD YOU IMMEDIATELY begin praying about what God wants you to do? God is very committed to having you involved in His great purposes for this world. Rest assured that as soon as you make yourself available to Him, He will take you at your word and put you to work.

In Matthew 9:36-38 (*THE MESSAGE*): *When (Jesus) looked out over the crowds, **his heart broke**. So confused and aimless they were, like sheep with no shepherd. "What a huge harvest!" he said to his disciples. "How few workers! On your knees and pray for harvest hands!"* Then in Matthew 10:1: *"**The prayer was no sooner prayed than it was answered.** Jesus called his twelve disciples and sent them into the ripe harvest fields"*

As you pray, the Lord will send you out right where you are and eventually to the unreached parts of the world.

John Ridgway
6th June 2018

Additional Reading

Herbert Hoefer in his book, "**Churchless Christianity**" (William Carey Library, 2001) notes that the number of high-caste Hindus worshipping Christ outside the existing church structure equaled the entire Protestant population of Madras, now Chennai.

Jerry Trousdale in "**Miraculous Movements**" (Nelson, 2012) details amazing stories of huge movements of the gospel in Africa and Asia fueled by intensive prayer and focusing on Jesus and His kingdom.

David Garrison in "**A Wind in the House of Islam**" (WIG Take Resources, 2014) states that in 70 separate locations in 29 nations, large gospel movements are happening in the Muslim world resulting in 7 million new Muslim background believers. This is in spite of almost no response for over 1300 years.

Another outstanding book is "**Understanding Insider Movements**" edited by Harley Talman and John Jay Travis (William Carey Library, 2015). It is a classic textbook drawing on more than 40 scholars and practitioners and is an outstanding effort to understand what is happening in our time in history. It lists the evidence for many of these movements, examining why these movements occur today as we seek to bring the Good News of the Kingdom of God to the unreached communities of the world.

About the Author

John Ridgway holds a PhD in Solid State Physics from the University of NSW, Australia. He was an industrial consultant for 32 years in India, Singapore, Malaysia and the USA. He has also been a coach to those involved in apostolic (pioneering) ministries and continues in this role right up to the present time. He and his wife Ruth and their two children lived and worked in India for 18 years. Their two children were born in India where John was teaching and undertaking research at India's top Graduate school called the Indian Institute of Science in the department of Physics in Bangalore and also working for several Australian and American multinationals. John continued this role in Singapore for 2 years and in Malaysia for 7 years. He was also the personal advisor to the Thai Royal Family at the request of the governments of Thailand and Australia. John also has made extensive visits to Japan over 10 years.

Contact him at: john@johnridgway.org

Website: www.johnridgway.org

Made in the USA
Monee, IL
04 May 2020